PUFFIN BOOKS

Edited by Eleanor Graham

PS121

A PUFFIN QUARTET OF POETS

This unusual anthology contains a selection of poems from the work of only four poets, but four of the finest who are writing verse for children today. A substantial amount from the work of each is given, enough to show their individual quality and special characteristics. The quartet is made up of Eleanor Farjeon, James Reeves, E. V. Rieu, and Ian Serraillier. There are brief biographical notes and a short introduction to each section suggesting how these poets go to work. Their methods of approach to verse-making proved, in fact, to be so diverse that together they cast much interesting light on the whole subject of composition.

A
PUFFIN
QUARTET
of
POETS

A PUFFIN QUARTET OF POETS

Eleanor Farjeon

James Reeves

E. V. Rieu

Ian Serraillier

SELECTED WITH INTRODUCTORY NOTES BY
ELEANOR GRAHAM
DECORATED WITH WOOD-ENGRAVINGS BY
DIANA BLOOMFIELD

PENGUIN BOOKS

Penguin Books Ltd, Harmondsworth, Middlesex

U.S.A.: Penguin Books Inc., 3300 Clipper Mill Road, Baltimore 11, Md

AUSTRALIA: Penguin Books Pty Ltd, 762 Whitehorse Road,
Mitcham, Victoria

—

This selection first published in Puffin Books 1958

—

Made and printed in Great Britain
by The Campfield Press,
St Albans

Contents

E. V. RIEU

IAN SERRAILLIER

Preface

This anthology of four poets started as an idea to gather into one volume enough of four modern writers to show the special qualities and characteristics of each. These proved to be so diverse as to show four quite different approaches to verse-making. A brief account of their methods, culled in every case from the poets themselves, forms a prefatory note at the beginning of each section.

Acknowledgements

I should like to thank very warmly all those
who have co-operated so generously to make
this volume possible: Eleanor Farjeon, who
allowed us to choose freely among all her
published work; Dr E. V. Rieu, for permission to use some unpublished poems as well
as to include poems from his *Cuckoo Calling*;
the Oxford University Press for permission
to include poems from Ian Serraillier's
Thomas and the Sparrow, *The Monster Horse*,
The Ballad of Kon-Tiki, and *Everest Climbed*,
and from James Reeves's *The Blackbird in the
Lilac*; and Messrs William Heinemann for
permission to include poems from James
Reeves's *The Wandering Moon*.

Eleanor Farjeon

Eleanor Farjeon is a member of a well-known literary family. She was born in Buckingham Street, off the Strand, in 1881. Her father was the popular novelist, B. L. Farjeon, and on her American mother's side, she was the grand-daughter of the famous actor, Joseph Jefferson. Her three brothers, Harry, Joe Jefferson, and Herbert, were all distinguished in their respective professions – music, novel-writing, dramatic criticism, and the writing of intimate revues.

She began to write tales and verses and fairy plays from the age of six, and at seven was writing them on her father's typewriter. During the first world war, she lived in a cowman's cottage in Sussex, and wrote *Martin Pippin in the Apple-Orchard*. This had instant success, and launched her on her career of fantastic fiction, verse of all sorts, and many books for children. Ten years later, she was collaborating in various ways with her brother Herbert, especially in plays with music which she found and rearranged from old sources. Their first hit was 'The Two Bouquets', for which they invented a Victorian romance, and their last completed collaboration before Herbert's death in 1945 was 'The Glass Slipper' which Robert Donat produced during the war.

In 1955 Eleanor Farjeon was awarded the Carnegie Medal for her collection of children's tales, *The Little Bookroom* (Oxford, 1955), and shortly afterwards this book received also the first award of the International Hans Andersen Medal.

She is now seventy-seven years of age, and the rest of her writing years will be spent on her Memoirs in several volumes.

ELEANOR FARJEON *is essentially a poet who writes from inspiration. Ideas come to her faster than she can deal with them. 'I was singing songs before I could write, even before I could speak,' she said once, 'as soon as I could guide a pencil, I began to write them.' And so, for half her life, 'song making' has been her 'trade'. She expresses herself more easily, more naturally, in 'running rhyme than plodding prose'. (The words are again her own.)*

Her verse is all born like that, as songs, alive and singing their own tunes in her head. The inspiration may come as a flashing vision of beauty, or truth, or emotion. It may arise out of things seen, heard, or held in the hand, or equally, out of some intuition of things not to be apprehended by the five physical senses. It is a sudden brilliant awareness, evoking all that is creative in her to receive and hold, to turn about and make over, an idea or impression or insight, into that new state which is a poem.

It is naturally important for her always to have a pencil and a scrap of paper handy, for, even if it means stopping on an island half-way across a busy street, she has to capture and set on paper enough of the idea in its particular mood and music before the colours fade.

Her work is rarely built up stone by stone on any small foundation. Still more rarely – if ever – can she sit down and deliberately set herself to write a poem.

These 'ideas' which flood her mind so constantly are not really windfalls from outside, but rather the fruit of her own perception and insight, the distillation of all she has learned and savoured about life, people, and all things lovely. Also, her natural impulse to share all she has is so strong, so generous, that it has a special significance in the warm vitality of her work. Meeting her, one feels for the moment alive in her life. Reading her verse has something of the same effect.

Good-morning now.
Wake, body,
Wake, mind!
Work, play,
Seek, find,
Eat breakfast,
Dinner too,
Wash, brush,
Sing, dance, and do!
Good-morning now.

How Many Cherries?

How many cherries
Have you got?
Eat up your cherries
On the spot,
Count your cherry-stones,
Learn your lot,
Are you lucky
Or are you not?

Some time! some time!
When will it be?
It might be winter,
It might be spring,
With snow on the ground
Or fruit on the tree,
Some time! some time!
When will it be?

Some one! some one!
What is he like?
Perhaps a coal-man,
Perhaps a king.
Will he come on a horse
Or a motor-bike?
Some one! some one!
What is he like?

Somewhere! somewhere!
Oh, but where?
In a hollow
Or on a height?
Over the water?
At the fair?
Somewhere! somewhere!
Oh, but where?

Some time! some time!
When will it be?
It might be morning,
It might be night,
With the sun in the sky
Or the moon on the sea –
Some time! some time!
When will it be?

Timothy went to Aragon
Riding on a weasel,
To ask the Dons for tarragon,
Tansy, thyme, and teasel.

The Dons they met in Aragon
Didn't like the weasel,
So Timothy got no tarragon,
Tansy, thyme, or teasel.

Joseph Fell a-Dreaming

Joseph fell a-dreaming.
He dreamed of sheaves of grain;
One stood upright like a tree,
The rest bowed down again.

His dreams came with the night
And he told them in the noon.
He dreamed of the eleven stars,
The sun and the moon.

The sun was his father,
The moon was his mother,
Of all the stars, the brightest star
Was Benjamin his brother.

A Wish

A glad New Year to all! –
Since many a tear,
Do what we can, must fall,
The greater need to wish a glad New Year.

Since lovely youth is brief,
O girl and boy,
And no one can escape a share of grief,
I wish you joy;

Since hate is with us still,
I wish men love;
I wish, since hovering hawks still strike to kill,
The coming of the dove;

And since the ghouls of terror and despair
Are still abroad,
I wish the world once more within the care
Of those who have seen God.

It was Long Ago

I'll tell you, shall I, something I remember?
Something that still means a great deal to me.
It was long ago.

A dusty road in summer I remember,
A mountain, and an old house, and a tree
That stood, you know,

Behind the house. An old woman I remember
In a red shawl with a grey cat on her knee
Humming under a tree.

She seemed the oldest thing I can remember,
But then perhaps I was not more than three.
It was long ago.

I dragged on the dusty road, and I remember
How the old woman looked over the fence at me
And seemed to know

How it felt to be three, and called out, I remember
'Do you like bilberries and cream for tea?'
I went under the tree

And while she hummed, and the cat purred, I remember
How she filled a saucer with berries and cream for me
So long ago,

Such berries and such cream as I remember
I never had seen before, and never see
To-day, you know.

And that is almost all I can remember,
The house, the mountain, the grey cat on her knee,
Her red shawl, and the tree,

And the taste of the berries, the feel of the sun I remember,
And the smell of everything that used to be
So long ago,

Till the heat on the road outside again I remember,
And how the long dusty road seemed to have for me
No end, you know.

That is the farthest thing I can remember.
It won't mean much to you. It does to me.
Then I grew up, you see.

Tailor

I saw a little Tailor sitting stitch, stitch, stitching
Cross-legged on the floor of his kitch, kitch, kitchen.
His thumbs and his fingers were so nim, nim, nimble
With his wax and his scissors and his thim, thim, thimble.

His silk and his cotton he was thread, thread, threading
For a gown and a coat for a wed, wed, wedding,
His needle flew as swift as a swal, swal, swallow,
And his spools and his reels had to fol, fol, follow.

He hummed as he worked a merry dit, dit, ditty:
'The Bride is as plump as she's pret, pret, pretty,
I wouldn't have her taller or short, short, shorter,
She can laugh like the falling of wat, wat, water,

'She can put a cherry-pie, togeth, geth, gether,
She can dance as light as a feath, feath, feather,
She can sing as sweet as a fid, fid, fiddle,
And she's only twenty inches round the mid, mid,
    middle.'

The happy little Tailor went on stitch, stitch, stitching
The black and the white in his kitch, kitch, kitchen.
He will wear the black one, she will wear the white one,
And the knot the Parson ties will be a tight, tight, tight
    one.

Missy Sinkins

Hey, Missy Sinkins,
Little Missy Sinkins,
In your pretty petticoats all cut in
    frilly pinkin's,
Here you come a-tiptoeing along
    the garden border
Like a ballerina with her snowy
    skirts in order.

They call you Mrs Sinkins –
Stuffy-Nonsense! pooh!
Nobody called Sinkins
Went and married you!
If any Mr Sinkins
Whispered: Name the Day!
You'd only shake your fluffy skirts at him,
And dance away.

Yes, Missy Sinkins,
I know you're Missy Sinkins,
Girlishly enjoying still your peekin's
    and your prinkin's,
Goffering your crumpled skirts, putting
    off the kisses,
Laughing No no no no no! I will not
    be a Mrs!

From Victoria I can go
To Pevensey Level and Piddinghoe,
Open Winkins and Didling Hill,
Three Cups Corner and Selsey Bill.
I'm the happiest one in all the nation
When my train runs out of Victoria Station.

But O the day when I come to town
From Ditchling Beacon and Duncton Down,
Bramber Castle and Wisborough Green,
Cissbury Ring and Ovingdean!
I'm the sorriest one in all the nation
When my train runs into Victoria Station.

Long Man of Wilmington

You Long Long Man of Wilmington,
How long have you been there? –
Before your grandsire's grandsire's grandsire's
Grandsire's sire was seen there.

You Long Long Man of Wilmington,
How long will you be there? –
Until your grandson's grandson's grandson's
Grandson's son see me there.

Sailor

My sweetheart's a Sailor,
He sails on the sea,
When he comes home
He brings presents for me;
Coral from China,
Silks from Siam,
Parrots and pearls
From Seringapatam,
Silver from Mexico,
Gold from Peru,
Indian feathers
From Kalamazoo,
Scents from Sumatra,
Mantillas from Spain,
A fisherman's float
From the waters of Maine,
Reindeers from Lapland,
Ducks from Bombay,
A unicorn's horn
From the Land of Cathay –
Isn't it lucky
For someone like me
To marry a Sailor
Who sails on the sea!

The Tide in the River

The tide in the river,
The tide in the river,
The tide in the river runs deep,
I saw a shiver
Pass over the river
As the tide turned in its sleep.

My wedding-gown's cotton,
    My wedding-gown's cheap,
It's crisper than sea-foam
    And whiter than sheep,
Printed with daisies
    In yellow and green,
A prettier wedding-gown
    Never was seen!
Light-heart and light-foot
    I'll walk into church
As straight and as slim
    As a silvery birch,
And after my wedding
    I never will lay
Like ladies my wedding-gown
    Lightly away.
I'll wash it in soapsuds
    As fresh as when new,
And rinse it in rainwater
    Softer than dew,
And peg it on Saturdays
    High on the line,
And wear it on Sundays
    Full of sunshine.
My wedding-gown's cotton,
    It cost me a crown,

Was ever girl wed in
    A commoner gown? –
As birds in the branches,
    As flowers on the green,
The commonest wedding-gown
    Ever was seen!

Mrs Malone
Lived hard by a wood
All on her lonesome
As nobody should.
With her crust on a plate
And her pot on the coal
And none but herself
To converse with, poor soul.
In a shawl and a hood
She got sticks out-o'-door,
On a bit of old sacking
She slept on the floor,
And nobody, nobody
Asked how she fared
Or knew how she managed,
For nobody cared.
   Why make a pother
   About an old crone?
   What for should they bother
   With Mrs Malone?

One Monday in winter
With snow on the ground
So thick that a footstep
Fell without sound,
She heard a faint frostbitten
Peck on the pane

And went to the window
To listen again.
There sat a cock-sparrow
Bedraggled and weak,
With half-open eyelid
And ice on his beak.
She threw up the sash
And she took the bird in,
And mumbled and fumbled it
Under her chin.
  'Ye're all of a smother,
   Ye're fair overblown!
   I've room fer another,'
   Said Mrs Malone.

Come Tuesday while eating
Her dry morning slice
With the sparrow a-picking
('Ain't company nice!')
She heard on her doorpost
A curious scratch,
And there was a cat
With its claw on the latch.
It was hungry and thirsty
And thin as a lath,
It mewed and it mowed
On the slithery path.
She threw the door open
And warmed up some pap,
And huddled and cuddled it

In her old lap.
  'There, there, little brother,
    Ye poor skin-an'-bone,
    There's room fer another,'
  Said Mrs Malone.

Come Wednesday while all of them
Crouched on the mat
With a crumb for the sparrow,
A sip for the cat,
There was wailing and whining
Outside in the wood,
And there sat a vixen
With six of her brood.
She was haggard and ragged
And worn to a shred,
And her half-dozen babies
Were only half-fed,
But Mrs Malone, crying
'My! ain't they sweet!'
Happed them and lapped them
And gave them to eat.
  'You warm yerself, mother,
    Ye're cold as a stone!
    There's room fer another,'
  Said Mrs Malone.

Come Thursday a donkey
Stepped in off the road
With sores on his withers

From bearing a load.
Come Friday when icicles
Pierced the white air
Down from the mountainside
Lumbered a bear.
For each she had something,
If little, to give –
'Lord knows, the poor critters
Must all of 'em live.'
She gave them her sacking,
Her hood and her shawl,
Her loaf and her teapot –
She gave them her all.
  'What with one thing and t'other
  Me fambily's grown,
  And there's room fer another,'
  Said Mrs Malone.

Come Saturday evening
When time was to sup
Mrs Malone
Had forgot to sit up.
The cat said *meeow*,
And the sparrow said *peep*,
The vixen, *she's sleeping*,
The bear, *let her sleep*.
On the back of the donkey
They bore her away,
Through trees and up mountains
Beyond night and day,

Till come Sunday morning
They brought her in state
Through the last cloudbank
As far as the Gate.
  'Who is it,' asked Peter,
  'You have with you there?'
  And donkey and sparrow,
  Cat, vixen and bear

Exclaimed, 'Do you tell us
Up here she's unknown?
It's our mother, God bless us!
It's Mrs Malone
Whose havings were few
And whose holding was small
And whose heart was so big
It had room for us all.'
Then Mrs Malone
Of a sudden awoke,
She rubbed her two eyeballs
And anxiously spoke:
'Where am I, to goodness,
And what do I see?
My dears, let's turn back,
This ain't no place fer me!'
  But Peter said, 'Mother
  Go in to the Throne.
  There's room for another
  One, Mrs Malone.'

Inside

A bellyful and the fire,
And him in his old suit,
And me with my heart's desire,
My head across his foot.

And I doze. And he reads.
And the clock ticks slow.
And, though he never heeds,
He knows, and I know.

Presently, without look,
His hand will feel to tug
My ear, his eyes on book,
Mine upon the rug.

*C*at!
Scat!
Atter her, atter her,
Sleeky flatterer,
Spitfire chatterer,
Scatter her, scatter her
      Off her mat!
      Wuff!
      Wuff!
      Treat her rough!
Git her, git her,
Whiskery spitter!
Catch her, catch her,
Green-eyed scratcher!
      Slathery
      Slithery
      Hisser,
      Don't miss her!
Run till you're dithery,
      Hithery
      Thithery
      Pfitts! pfitts!
      How she spits!
      Spitch! Spatch!
      Can't she scratch!
Scritching the bark
Of the sycamore-tree,

She's reached her ark
And's hissing at me
Pfitts! pfitts!
Wuff! wuff!
Scat,
Cat!
That's
That!

Rise harrow, rake harrow,
After the plough.
Haysel-time, harvest-time,
Rest harrow now.

Wheelbarrow

He dumped her in the wheelbarrow
   And trundled her away!
How he chaffed and how she laughed
   On their wedding-day!

He bumped her through the garden-gate,
   He bounced her down the lane!
Then he reeled and then she squealed,
   And off they bounced again.

He jiggled her across the ditch,
   He joggled her through the holt!
He stubbed his toe and she cried O!
   Whenever she got a jolt.

He wiggled her up the bridle-path,
   He woggled her through the street –
Down he stumbled! down she tumbled,
   Right at the Parson's feet!

O my sweet Nightingales, why are you dumb again?
O my blue Violets, when will you come again?
O my brown Bees in the yellow Lime-Trees,
Humble-Bees, Bumble-Bees, when will you hum again?

The Elm-Tree

One November morning clean and cold
The elm-tree still was heavy with her gold,
Though beech and oak and aspen stripped and bare
Lifted their leafless branches in the air.

Then something happened, and her golden dress
The noble elm shook from her nakedness;
Yes, in a single hour, like a great rain,
She gave back all her leaves to earth again.

Keep Still

Look, and keep very still,
Still as a tree,
And if you do you will
Presently see
The doe come down to drink
Leading her fawn
Just as they did, I think,
In the first dawn.

Hark, not a sound, my dear,
Be quiet and hark,
And very soon you'll hear
The vixen bark,
And see her cubs at play
As I believe
They played in starlight grey
On the first eve.

Look, and keep very still.
Hark, not a sound!
The pretty creatures will
Soon be around,
At play and drink, as though
They drank and played
Cub, vixen, fawn and doe,
Ere men were made.

Cottage

When I live in a Cottage
I shall keep in my Cottage

Two different Dogs,
Three creamy Cows,
Four giddy Goats,
Five Pewter Pots
Six silver Spoons
Seven busy Beehives
Eight ancient Appletrees
Nine red Rosebushes
Ten teeming Teapots
Eleven chirping Chickens
Twelve cosy Cats with their kittenish Kittens and
One blessèd Baby in a Basket.

That's what I'll have when I live in my Cottage.

There was a yellow pumpkin
Born on a pumpkin-patch,
As clumsy as a 'potamus,
As coarse as cottage-thatch.
It longed to be a gooseberry,
A greengage, or a grape,
It longed to give another scent
And have another shape.
The roses looked askance at it,
The lilies looked away –
'This thing is neither fruit nor flower!'
Their glances seemed to say.

One shiny night of midsummer,
When even fairies poach,
A good one waved her wand and said,
'O Pumpkin! be a coach!'
A coach of gold! a coach of glass!
A coach with satin lined!
If you should seek a thousand years,
Such you would not find.
The Princess in her crystal shoes
Eager for the dance
Stepped inside the pumpkin-coach
And rolled to her romance.

The roses reached out after it,
The lilies looked its way –
'O that we were pumpkins too!'
Their glances seemed to say.

Keeping Christmas

How will you your Christmas keep?
Feasting, fasting, or asleep?
Will you laugh or will you pray,
Or will you forget the day?

Be it kept with joy or pray'r,
Keep of either some to spare;
Whatsoever brings the day,
Do not keep but give away.

For Them

Before you bid, for Christmas' sake,
   Your guests to sit at meat,
Oh please to save a little cake
   For them that have no treat.

Before you go down party-dressed
   In silver gown or gold,
Oh please to send a little vest
   To them that still go cold.

Before you give your girl and boy
   Gay gifts to be undone,
Oh please to spare a little toy
   To them that will have none.

Before you gather round the tree
   To dance the day about,
Oh please to give a little glee
   To them that go without.

Now good-night.
Fold up your clothes
As you were taught,
Fold your two hands,
Fold up your thought;
Day is the plough-land,
Night is the stream,
Day is for doing
And night is for dream.
Now good-night.

James Reeves

James Reeves was born at Harrow, Middlesex, on 1 July 1909, and was educated at Stowe and Jesus College, Cambridge. He has lived mainly in the country, in Buckinghamshire and Sussex, but has travelled abroad also. He is married and has three children, two girls and a boy.

He has taught and lectured to teachers, but in 1952 he gave that up to devote his time to writing and broadcasting. His hobbies are gardening, listening to the radio and gramophone, and going to concerts.

He has written two books of verse for children: *The Wandering Moon* (Heinemann, 1950) and *The Blackbird in the Lilac* (Oxford, 1952). His other books for children are: *English Fables and Fairy Stories* (Oxford Myths and Legend Series, 1953); *Pigeons and Princesses* (Stories, Heinemann, 1956); *Mulcaster Market and Other Plays* (Heinemann, 1951); *The King Who Took Sunshine* (A Play, Heinemann, 1954); *Prefabulous Animiles* (with Edward Ardizzone, Heinemann, 1957): and *A Health to John Patch* (A Ballad Opera for Children, Boosey & Hawkes). His plays have all been produced in schools, as has the Ballad Opera. Some of his poetry, and some of the English Fables have been broadcast in B.B.C. Children's Hour.

JAMES REEVES brings to his making of poetry a good deal of practical experience, and a mind informed on the subject by teaching and by lecturing to teachers. He has studied and observed children's natural tastes in poetry and their reactions to it. He had therefore certain positive aims and intentions when he began to compose.

Each of the two volumes from which these verses are taken was written in one piece, by concentrated effort and deliberate detachment from the affairs and conditions of the moment. It is worth recalling, in passing, that some of the most tender verses in A Child's Garden were written in a similar kind of abstraction, though for Robert Louis Stevenson it was not from choice, but owing to inescapable conditions created by sickness. A. A. Milne also worked in something of the same way, when he shut himself up in a summer-house during a wet August holiday to see whether he could write a book for children.

In each case there was a surrendering to, and a re-entering into, the world of childish impressions, emotions, reactions. So also James Reeves deliberately shut himself away to write his verses for children, thinking and feeling his way back into the core of childish experience, recapturing the emotional tone of those moments with an intensity which had something trance-like about it, getting the picture clear, allowing to develop the rhythmic form which nearly always sprang with it, ready made, into his mind.

The thing called inspiration was clearly at work in him, the experience and the emotion flowing spontaneously into a melodious form which was fitting. It is significant that, while he works carefully over verse for adult readers, he finds he can rarely revise what he has written for children.

He wrote each of these books in one brief, concentrated spell, making sometimes as many as three or four poems in a day. He keeps them simple and not too long, partly of necessity, for impaired eyesight renders more difficult the almost unending revision some writers are accustomed to.

Sometimes he sets himself a problem, for instance, to show some common experience in metaphorical form. That was how the poem The Sea is a Hungry Dog came to be written. Walking on the beach at Eastbourne, he felt the sea as a dog leaping upon the pebbles, a great grey dog with 'clashing teeth and shaggy jaws', gnawing the 'rumbling, tumbling stones' . . . and 'Bones, bones, bones, bones!' he heard the giant sea-dog moan.

Things to Remember

The buttercups in May,
The wild rose on the spray,
The poppy in the hay,

The primrose in the dell,
The freckled foxglove bell,
The honeysuckle's smell

Are things I would remember
When cheerless, raw November
Makes room for dark December.

Slowly

Slowly the tide creeps up the sand,
Slowly the shadows cross the land.
Slowly the cart-horse pulls his mile,
Slowly the old man mounts the stile.

Slowly the hands move round the clock,
Slowly the dew dries on the dock.
Slow is the snail – but slowest of all
The green moss spreads on the old brick wall.

.

Smooth and flat, grey, brown and white,
Winter and summer, noon and night,
Tumbling together for a thousand ages,
We ought to be wiser than Eastern sages.
But no doubt we stones are foolish as most,
So we don't say much on our stretch of coast.
Quiet and peaceful we mainly sit,
And when storms come up we grumble a bit.

Run a Little

Run a little this way,
  Run a little that!
Fine new feathers
  For a fine new hat.
A fine new hat
  For a lady fair –
Run around and turn about
  And jump in the air.

Run a little this way,
  Run a little that!
White silk ribbon
  For a black silk cat.
A black silk cat
  For the Lord Mayor's wife –
Run around and turn about
  And fly for your life!

Fireworks

They rise like sudden fiery flowers
    That burst upon the night,
Then fall to earth in burning showers
    Of crimson, blue, and white.

Like buds too wonderful to name,
    Each miracle unfolds,
And catherine-wheels begin to flame
    Like whirling marigolds.

Rockets and Roman candles make
    An orchard of the sky,
Whence magic trees their petals shake
    Upon each gazing eye.

Mr Tom Narrow

A scandalous man
    Was Mr Tom Narrow,
He pushed his grandmother
    Round in a barrow.
And he called out loud
    As he rang his bell,
'Grannies to sell!
    Old grannies to sell!'

The neighbours said,
    As they passed them by,
'This poor old lady
    We will not buy.
He surely must be
    A mischievous man
To try for to sell
    His own dear Gran.'

'Besides,' said another,
    'If you ask me,
She'd be very small use
    That I can see.'
'You're right,' said a third,
    'And no mistake –
A very poor bargain
    She'd surely make.'

So Mr Tom Narrow
  He scratched his head,
And he sent his grandmother
  Back to bed;
And he rang his bell
  Through all the town
Till he sold his barrow
  For half a crown.

Mrs Button

When Mrs Button, of a morning,
　　Comes creaking down the street,
You hear her old two black boots whisper
　　'Poor feet – poor feet – poor feet!'

When Mrs Button, every Monday,
　　Sweeps the chapel neat,
All down the long, hushed aisles they whisper
　　'Poor feet – poor feet – poor feet!'

Mrs Button after dinner
　　(It is her Sunday treat)
Sits down and takes her two black boots off
　　And rests her two poor feet.

A Pig Tale

Poor Jane Higgins,
She had five piggins,
And one got drowned in the Irish Sea.
Poor Jane Higgins,
She had four piggins,
And one flew over a sycamore tree.
Poor Jane Higgins,
She had three piggins,
And one was taken away for pork.
Poor Jane Higgins,
She had two piggins,
And one was sent to the Bishop of Cork.
Poor Jane Higgins,
She had one piggin,
And that was struck by a shower of hail,
So poor Jane Higgins,
She had no piggins,
And that's the end of my little pig tale.

Half the time they munched the grass, and all the
    time they lay
Down in the water-meadows, the lazy month of May,
        A-chewing,
        A-mooing,
     To pass the hours away.

    'Nice weather,' said the brown cow.
      'Ah,' said the white.
    'Grass is very tasty.'
      'Grass is all right.'

Half the time they munched the grass, and all the
    time they lay
Down in the water-meadows, the lazy month of May,
        A-chewing,
        A-mooing,
     To pass the hours away.

    'Rain coming,' said the brown cow.
      'Ah,' said the white.
    'Flies is very tiresome.'
      'Flies bite.'

Half the time they munched the grass, and all the
    time they lay
Down in the water-meadows, the lazy month of May,

          A-chewing,
          A-mooing,
     To pass the hours away.

        'Time to go,' said the brown cow.
          'Ah,' said the white.
        'Nice chat.' 'Very pleasant.'
          'Night.' 'Night.'

Half the time they munched the grass, and all the
     time they lay
Down in the water-meadows, the lazy month of May,
          A-chewing,
          A-mooing,
     To pass the hours away.

Spells

I dance and dance without any feet –
This is the spell of the ripening wheat.

With never a tongue I've a tale to tell –
This is the meadow-grasses' spell.

I give you health without any fee –
This is the spell of the apple-tree.

I rhyme and riddle without any book –
This is the spell of the bubbling brook.

Without any legs I run for ever –
This is the spell of the mighty river.

I fall for ever and not at all –
This is the spell of the waterfall.

Without a voice I roar aloud –
This is the spell of the thunder-cloud.

No button or seam has my white coat –
This is the spell of the leaping goat.

I can cheat strangers with never a word –
This is the spell of the cuckoo-bird.

We have tongues in plenty but speak no names –
This is the spell of the fiery flames.

The creaking door has a spell to riddle –
I play a tune without any fiddle.

Waiting

Waiting, waiting, waiting
  For the party to begin;
Waiting, waiting, waiting
  For the laughter and din;
Waiting, waiting, waiting
  With hair just so
And clothes trim and tidy
  From top-knot to toe.
The floor is all shiny,
  The lights are ablaze;
There are sweetmeats in plenty
  And cakes beyond praise.
Oh the games and dancing,
  The tricks and the toys,
The music and the madness
  The colour and noise!
Waiting, waiting, waiting
  For the first knock on the door –
Was ever such waiting,
  Such waiting before?

Queer Things

'Very, very queer things have been happening to me
    In some of the places where I've been.
I went to the pillar-box this morning with a letter
    And a hand came out and took it in.

'When I got home again, I thought I'd have
    A glass of spirits to steady myself;
And I take my bible oath, but that bottle and glass
    Came a-hopping down off the shelf.

'No, no, I says, I'd better take no spirits,
    And I sat down to have a cup of tea;
And blowed if my old pair of carpet-slippers
    Didn't walk across the carpet to me!

'So I took my newspaper and went into the park,
    And looked round to see no one was near,
When a voice right out of the middle of the paper
    Started reading the news bold and clear!

'Well, I guess there's some magician out to help me,
    So perhaps there's no need for alarm;
And if I manage not to anger him,
    Why should he do me any harm?'

The Two Mice

There met two mice at Scarborough
    Beside the rushing sea,
The one from Market Harborough,
    The other from Dundee.

They shook their feet, they clapped their hands,
    And twirled their tails about;
They danced all day upon the sands
    Until the stars peeped out.

'I'm much fatigued,' the one mouse sighed,
    'And ready for my tea.'
'Come hame awa',' the other cried,
    'And tak' a crumb wi' me.'

They slept awhile, and then next day
    Across the moors they went;
But sad to say, they lost their way
    And came to Stoke-on-Trent.

And there it soon began to rain,
    At which they cried full sore:
'If ever we get home again,
    We'll not go dancing more.'

Roundabout

At midsummer fair on a galloping pony
We saw the last of little Tony.
He spurred her sides and said 'Hurroo!'
And over the heads of the crowd he flew.
Said the roundabout man, 'Now don't get tragic –
That boy'll come back, the horse is magic!'
Up went Tony in the blue, blue air,
Right over the top of midsummer fair.
Till the roundabout music he heard no more,
And he set his course for the southern shore.
He saw the houses, row on row,
And he heard the cocks in the farms below.
Trees and rivers went sliding by
As the pony sailed through the blue, blue sky.
He saw the ships and the coast of France
And sailor-boys in a hornpipe dance.
He passed strange birds which he shouted to,
And away to the south he flew and flew.
Night came on and another day
And still he flew to the south away.
On and on at a galloping speed
Went little Tony and his roundabout steed.
Churches he saw and castles and towns,
Mountains and forests, dales and downs.
They crossed the Mediterranean Sea
And they came to the coast of Afrikee.
And there were palm-trees and black men bare,

All hot and hazy in the tropical air.
And lone grey mountains and deserts brown
And giant cataracts tumbling down,
Giraffes and lions and chimpanzees
And monkeys swinging among the trees.
He never felt hungry, did little Tony,
Sitting astride his magic pony,
But after a while the marvellous beast
Changed its course and made for the east,
And they came to an island in the sea
Not far from the shores of Afrikee.
So they lighted down and soon they stood
On a wild hillside by a little wood.
After a while a native came
Who gave them food and told them his name.
And there they'll stay for a year or more
Where never a white boy stayed before.
There in the sun lives little Tony
With the friendly natives and the magic pony.
One of these days he will say good-bye
And rise aloft in the blue, blue sky,
And gallop away through the air once more
Till he lands at last on his native shore.
So you see what marvellous things and rare
Can chance to a boy at midsummer fair.

Rabbit and Lark

'Under the ground
  It's rumbly and dark
And interesting,'
  Said Rabbit to Lark.

Said Lark to Rabbit,
  'Up in the sky
There's plenty of room
  And it's airy and high.'

'Under the ground
  It's warm and dry.
Won't you live with me?'
  Was Rabbit's reply.

'The air's so sunny.
  I wish you'd agree,'
Said the little Lark,
  'To live with me.'

But under the ground
  And up in the sky,
Larks can't burrow
  Nor rabbits fly.

So Skylark over
  And Rabbit under
They had to settle
  To live asunder.

And often these two friends
Meet with a will
For a chat together
On top of the hill.

The Snail

At sunset, when the night-dews fall,
Out of the ivy on the wall
With horns outstretched and pointed tail
Comes the grey and noiseless snail.
On ivy stems she clambers down,
Carrying her house of brown.
Safe in the dark, no greedy eye
Can her tender body spy,
While she herself, a hungry thief,
Searches out the freshest leaf.
She travels on as best she can
Like a toppling caravan.

Animals' Houses

Of animals' houses
   Two sorts are found –
Those which are square ones
   And those which are round.

Square is a hen-house,
   A kennel, a sty:
Cows have square houses
   And so have I.

A snail's shell is curly,
   A bird's nest round;
Rabbits have twisty burrows
   Underground.

But the fish in the bowl
   And the fish at sea –
Their houses are round
   As a house can be.

The Old Wife and the Ghost

There was an old wife and she lived all alone
　　In a cottage not far from Hitchin:
And one bright night, by the full moon light,
　　Comes a ghost right into her kitchen.

About that kitchen neat and clean
　　The ghost goes pottering round.
But the poor old wife is deaf as a boot
　　And so hears never a sound.

The ghost blows up the kitchen fire,
　　As bold as bold can be;
He helps himself from the larder shelf,
　　But never a sound hears she.

He blows on his hands to make them warm,
　　And whistles aloud 'Whee-hee!'
But still as a sack the old soul lies
　　And never a sound hears she.

From corner to corner he runs about,
　　And into the cupboard he peeps;
He rattles the door and bumps on the floor,
　　But still the old wife sleeps.

Jangle and bang go the pots and pans,
　　As he throws them all around;
And the plates and mugs and dishes and jugs,
　　He flings them all to the ground.

Madly the ghost tears up and down
　　And screams like a storm at sea;
And at last the old wife stirs in her bed –
　　And it's 'Drat those mice,' says she.

Then the first cock crows and morning shows
　　And the troublesome ghost's away.
But oh! what a pickle the poor wife sees
　　When she gets up next day.

'Them's tidy big mice,' the old wife thinks,
　　And off she goes to Hitchin,
And a tidy big cat she fetches back
　　To keep the mice from her kitchen.

Stocking and shirt
  Can trip and prance,
Though nobody's in them
  To make them dance.
See how they waltz
  Or minuet,
Watch the petticoat
  Pirouette.
This is the dance
  Of stocking and shirt,
When the wind puts on
  The white lace skirt.
Old clothes and young clothes
  Dance together,
Twirling and whirling
  In the mad March weather.
'Come!' cries the wind,
  To stocking and shirt.
'Away!' cries the wind
  To blouse and skirt.
Then clothes and wind
  All pull together,
Tugging like mad
  In the mad March weather.
Across the garden
  They suddenly fly

And over the far hedge
    High, high, high!
'Stop!' cries the housewife,
    But all too late,
Her clothes have passed
    The furthest gate.
They are gone for ever
    In the bright blue sky,
And only the handkerchiefs
    Wave good-bye.

Mick my mongrel-O
Lives in a bungalow,
Painted green with a round doorway.
With an eye for cats
And a nose for rats
He lies on his threshold half the day.
He buries his bones
By the rockery stones,
And never, oh never, forgets the place.
Ragged and thin
From his tail to his chin,
He looks at you with a sideways face.
Dusty and brownish,
Wicked and clownish,
He'll win no prize at the County Show.
But throw him a stick,
And up jumps Mick,
And right through the flower-beds see him go!

The Footprint

Poor Crusoe saw with fear-struck eyes
    The footprint on the shore –
Oh! what is this that shines so clear
    Upon the bathroom floor?

The Sea

The sea is a hungry dog,
Giant and grey.
He rolls on the beach all day.
With his clashing teeth and shaggy jaws
Hour upon hour he gnaws
The rumbling, tumbling stones,
And 'Bones, bones, bones, bones!'
The giant sea-dog moans,
Licking his greasy paws.

And when the night wind roars
And the moon rocks in the stormy cloud,
He bounds to his feet and snuffs and sniffs,
Shaking his wet sides over the cliffs,
And howls and hollos long and loud.

But on quiet days in May or June,
When even the grasses on the dune
Play no more their reedy tune,
With his head between his paws
He lies on the sandy shores,
So quiet, so quiet, he scarcely snores.

Village Sounds

Lie on this green and close your eyes –
   A busy world you'll hear
Of noises high and low, and loud
   And soft, and far and near.

Amidst the squawking geese and ducks,
   And hens that cluck and croon,
The rooster on the dung-hill sings
   His shrill, triumphant tune.

A watch-dog barks to scare away
   Some sudden passer-by;
The dog wakes Mrs Goodman's Jane
   And she begins to cry.

And now the crying babe is still,
   You hear young blacksmith George
Din-dinning on his anvil bright
   Far off in his black forge.

Then on his tinkling cycle comes
   The postman with his load,
And motor-buses sound their horns
   Upon the London Road.

Sometimes a hay-cart rumbles past,
   The old sow grunts and stirs,
And in John Farrow's timber-yard
   The engine throbs and whirrs.

Just across there the schoolroom stands,
   And from the open door
You hear the sound of 'Billy Boy'
   Or else of four times four.

At half-past-three a sudden noise –
   The children come from school,
And shouting to the meadow run
   To play beside the pool.

And then, when all these sounds are still
   In the hot afternoon,
As you lie on the quiet green
   You'll hear my favourite tune.

Down from the green boughs overhead
   The gentlest murmurs float,
As hour by hour the pigeon coos
   His soft contented note.

Explorers

The furry moth explores the night,
　　The fish discover cities drowned,
And moles and worms and ants explore
　　The many cupboards underground.

The soaring lark explores the sky,
　　And gulls explore the stormy seas.
The busy squirrel rummages
　　Among the attics of the trees.

The Intruder

Two-boots in the forest walks,
Pushing through the bracken stalks.

Vanishing like a puff of smoke,
Nimbletail flies up the oak.

Longears helter-skelter shoots
Into his house among the roots.

At work upon the highest bark,
Tapperbill knocks off to hark.

Painted-wings through sun and shade
Flounces off along the glade.

Not a creature lingers by,
When clumping Two-boots comes to pry.

Little Fan

'I don't like the look of little Fan, mother,
  I don't like her looks a little bit.
Her face – well, it's not exactly different,
  But there's something wrong with it.

'She went down to the sea-shore yesterday,
  And she talked to somebody there,
Now she won't do anything but sit
  And comb out her yellowy hair.

'Her eyes are shiny and she sings, mother,
  Like nobody ever sang before.
Perhaps they gave her something queer to eat,
  Down by the rocks on the shore.

'Speak to me, speak, little Fan dear,
  Aren't you feeling very well?
Where have you been and what are you singing,
  And what's that seaweedy smell?

'Where did you get that shiny comb, love,
  And those pretty coral beads so red?
Yesterday you had two legs, I'm certain,
  But now there's something else instead.

'I don't like the looks of little Fan, mother,
  You'd best go and close the door.
Watch now, or she'll be gone for ever
  To the rocks by the brown sandy shore.'

Oh, grim and gloomy,
So grim and gloomy
Are the caves beneath the sea.
Oh, rare but roomy
And bare and boomy,
Those salt sea caverns be.

Oh, slim and slimy
Or grey and grimy
Are the animals of the sea.
Salt and oozy
And safe and snoozy
The caves where those animals be.

Hark to the shuffling,
Huge and snuffling,
Ravenous, cavernous, great sea-beasts!
But fair and fabulous,
Tintinnabulous,
Gay and fabulous are their feasts.

Ah, but the queen of the sea,
The querulous, perilous sea!
How the curls of her tresses
The pearls on her dresses,
Sway and swirl in the waves,
How cosy and dozy,

How sweet ring a-rosy
Her bower in the deep-sea caves!

Oh, rare but roomy
And bare and boomy
Those caverns under the sea,
And grave and grandiose,
Safe and sandiose
The dens of her denizens be.

The Magic Seeds

There was an old woman who sowed a corn seed,
And from it there sprouted a tall yellow weed.
She planted the seeds of the tall yellow flower,
And up sprang a blue one in less than an hour.
The seed of the blue one she sowed in a bed,
And up sprang a tall tree with blossoms of red.
And high in the treetop there sang a white bird,
And his song was the sweetest that ever was heard.
The people they came from far and from near,
The song of the little white bird for to hear.

The Wind

I can get through a doorway without any key,
And strip the leaves from the great oak tree.

I can drive storm-clouds and shake tall towers,
Or steal through a garden and not wake the flowers.

Seas I can move and ships I can sink;
I can carry a house-top or the scent of a pink.

When I am angry I can rave and riot;
And when I am spent, I lie quiet as quiet.

There was a man of Uriconium
Who played a primitive harmonium,
Inventing, to relieve his tedium,
Melodies high, low, and medium,
And standing on his Roman cranium
Amidst a bed of wild geranium,
Better known as pelargonium,
Since with odium his harmonium
Was received in Uriconium.

Boating

Gently the river bore us
   Beneath the morning sky,
Singing, singing, singing
Its reedy, quiet tune
   As we went floating by;
And all the afternoon
   In our small boat we lay
Rocking, rocking, rocking
   Under the willows grey.

When into bed that evening
   I climbed, it seemed a boat
Was softly rocking, rocking,
Rocking me to sleep,
   And I was still afloat.
I heard the grey leaves weep
   And whisper round my bed,
The river singing, singing,
   Singing through my head.

Time to go home!
  Says the great steeple clock.
Time to go home!
  Says the gold weathercock.
Down sinks the sun
  In the valley to sleep;
Lost are the orchards
  In blue shadows deep.
Soft falls the dew
  On cornfield and grass;
Through the dark trees
  The evening airs pass:
Time to go home,
  They murmur and say;
Birds to their homes
  Have all flown away.
Nothing shines now
  But the gold weathercock.
Time to go home!
  Says the great steeple clock.

Trees in the Moonlight

Trees in the moonlight stand
   Still as a steeple,
And so quiet they seem like ghosts
   Of country people –

Dead farmers and their wives
   Of long, long ago,
Haunting the countryside
   They used to know;

Old gossips and talkers
   With tongues gone still;
Ploughmen rooted in the land
   They used to till;

Old carters and harvesters,
   Their wheels long rotten;
Old maids whose very names
   Time has forgotten.

Ghosts are they hereabouts;
   Them the moon sees,
Dark and still in the fields
   Like sleeping trees.

Long nights in autumn
   Hear them strain and cry,
Torn with a wordless sorrow
   As the gale sweeps by.

Spring makes fresh buds appear
 On the old boughs,
As if it could to their old wishes
 These ghosts arouse.

Trees in the summer night
 By moonlight linger on
So quiet they seem like ghosts
 Of people gone,

And it would be small wonder
 If at break of day
They heard the far-off cock-crow
 And fled away.

E. V. Rieu, C.B.E., HON. LITT.D.(Leeds), F.R.S.L., was born in London in 1887; he was educated at St Paul's School and Balliol College, Oxford. He is now Academic and Literary Adviser to Methuen & Co. Ltd and Editor of Penguin Classics.

He has lived mainly in London, though from 1912 to 1919 he was in India as Manager for the Oxford University Press. In 1923 he became Educational Manager for Methuen, and Managing Director in 1933 (until 1936). His hobbies are carpentry, mountains, and petrology. His publications include *A Book of Latin Poetry* (Methuen, 1925); *Cuckoo Calling* (Methuen, 1933); and, in Penguin Classics, translations of *The Odyssey* (1945); *Virgil's Pastoral Poems* (1949); *The Iliad* (1950); and *The Four Gospels* (1952).

DR E. V. RIEU'S *verse is very much a busy man's hobby, the delight of quiet hours, insinuating itself delicately between him and his preoccupations with the classics and the art of translation. He finds relaxation and refreshment in experimenting with rhythms and weaving into them unexpected effects of levity. They have come from his pen at long intervals throughout his distinguished career as publisher, editor of Penguin Classics, and translator of (among others)* The Odyssey, *and* The Four Gospels.

Inspiration comes to him as a phrase tumbling into his mind from nowhere, already dancing at its own pace, significant and suggestive enough to capture his attention. That phrase becomes the keystone round which the rest is built up. He toys with it, trying it this way and that, seeking the angle which best admits that humorous approach which, to Dr Rieu, represents the joke he likes to find under the surface of every situation.

He is a perfectionist, and probably never considers his work final and beyond improvement. Most of these verses have been kept beside him for years and brought out at long intervals for criticism and reflection, to be tried on the tongue to test their lightness and compactness, or in the hope of neatening some small point which has so far eluded him.

He thinks he writes verse only because in his heart he so greatly desires to do so, and that otherwise these key phrases would be turned to account in some other way. He finds his subjects in the domestic affairs of home, family, and pets – or in a more exotic and fanciful world of unicorns, penguins, hippopotamus, lynx, or flying fish – but all dance to his pipe.

The verses included here are from Cuckoo Calling, *except for the following which are printed for the first time:* The Paint Box, Two People, A Pair of Slippers, Rendez-vous with a Beetle, The Snake and the Snake-Charmer, The Hippopotamus's

Birthday, Meditations of a Tortoise, The Lament of the White Mouse, Soliloquy of a Tortoise, The White Rabbit, Night Thought of a Tortoise, Pirates on Funafuti, The Green Train, The Lady of Leigh, Cat's Funeral.

What Does it Matter?

What does it matter to you and me
Whether it's half past eight or three?
The nursery clock has just gone one;
And hark, the clock in the hall's begun!
But it must be wrong, for it's striking seven;
And there goes another one, on to eleven!
   And I think it's four,
    But it might be more –
Oh, what does it matter to you and me?
Let's have dinner and call it tea!
And we'll all go to bed and wake at three,
   For the Sun will be right in the morning.

The Lost Cat

She took a last and simple meal when there were
      none to see her steal –
    A jug of cream upon the shelf, a fish prepared
        for dinner;
And now she walks a distant street with delicately
      sandalled feet,
    And no one gives her much to eat or weeps to see
      her thinner.

O my belovèd come again, come back in joy, come
      back in pain,
    To end our searching with a mew, or with a purr
        our grieving;
And you shall have for lunch or tea whatever fish
      swim in the sea
    And all the cream that's meant for me – and not
      a word of thieving!

Mr Blob

My heart went out to Mr Blob
        the moment that we met,
And the manner of his coming
        is a thing I can't forget.
It fell upon a Sunday
        in the merry month of June,
Between a rainy morning
        and a rainy afternoon.

He didn't use the window,
        and he didn't use the door;
He never took his hat off,
        and he never touched the floor;
He didn't look as if he'd grown,
        like us: he just began,
And stood before us there,
        a simple English gentleman.

He wasn't very dandified
        or dainty in his dress,
But the absence of his trousers
        seemed to cause him no distress,
For the smile upon his features
        was a marvel to behold,
And underneath that buttoned vest
        there beat a heart of gold.

He wasn't long among us:
          all too little had been said
When a heavy hand descended
          on his inoffensive head,
And a Voice delivered judgement:
          'Mr Blob is far too stout;
He's a silly little fellow,
          and I mean to rub him out.'

MR BLOB

He didn't seem offended,
          but I think he must have heard,
For he rose up from the paper
          and he went without a word.
His boots and buttons only
          lingered on a little while,
And the last of him to vanish
          was the vestige of a smile.

O Mr Blob, the world would be
         a very pleasant place
If everyone resembled you
         in figure and in face.
If everybody went about
         with open arms like you
The stars would all be brighter
         and the sky a bluer blue.

My heart went out to Mr Blob
         the moment that we met,
And the sorrow of his going
         is a thing that haunts me yet;
For often when the clouds are low
         I sit at home and sob
To think that I shall see no more
         the face of Mr Blob.

The Paint Box

'Cobalt and umber and ultramarine,
Ivory black and emerald green –
What shall I paint to give pleasure to you?'
'Paint for me somebody utterly new.'

'I have painted you tigers in crimson and white.'
'The colours were good and you painted aright.'
'I have painted the cook and a camel in blue
And a panther in purple.' 'You painted them true.

Now mix me a colour that nobody knows,
And paint me a country where nobody goes.
And put in it people a little like you,
Watching a unicorn drinking the dew.'

Portrait of a House

The house that we live in was built in a place
That was once a mere cube of unoccupied space;
And the birds that flew through it and passed on their way
Would collide with a wall or a window to-day.

The rooms in the house are of medium size,
The sort that an ant would regard with surprise;
While a whale could express no opinion at all,
For his bulk would prevent him from passing the hall.

The stairs are arranged with such exquisite skill
That a person can climb or descend them at will;
And the absence of rain from the attics is proof
That the architect thought of supplying a roof.

Of the doors and the windows our only complaint
Is the fact that you can't see the wood for the paint:
A trouble with which we've decided to deal
By allowing the paint to continue to peel.

The chairs and the tables are perfectly tame,
And to speak of them harshly is rather a shame;
But nevertheless I am bound to remark
On their savage resistance when bumped in the dark.

In the kitchen, in spite of its tropical clime,
Two cats and a cook spend the whole of their time.
The cats have been known to meander about,
But the cook is a fixture and never goes out.

It is said that mysterious sounds may be heard
In the house when it's empty; but this is absurd.
If you've gone there to listen, it's clear to a dunce
That the house will have ceased to be empty at once.

We've a spare-room prepared for the casual guest,
But it really is not what the name would suggest;
For although it's a room, it is never to spare,
As someone or other is constantly there.

I have made it quite clear that our chosen abode
Is different from all of the rest in the road –
What a beautiful house for play, dinner and slumber!
And yet to the postman it's only a number.

Two People

Two people live in Rosamund,
   And one is very nice;
The other is devoted
   To every kind of vice –

To walking where the puddles are,
   And eating far too quick,
And saying words she shouldn't know,
   And wanting spoons to lick.

Two people live in Rosamund,
   And one (I say it twice)
Is very nice *and* very good:
   The other's only nice.

Sleeping in the big bed
    Rosamund; and, below,
An empty pair of slippers,
    Just where slippers go.

Very very quiet,
    And very very neat:
Anyone would *know* they came
    Off a good girl's feet.

Just a little lonely,
    Just a little sad,
Out upon the cold floor –
    Oh, anything but bad!

Never was a pair of
    Shoes so good as they –
But oh, the dance they'll lead her
    All the bouncing day!

Hall and Knight

OR

$$z + b + x = y + b + z$$

When he was young his cousins
        used to say of Mr Knight:
'This boy will write an Algebra –
        or looks as if he might.'
And sure enough, when Mr Knight
        had grown to be a man,
He purchased pen and paper
        and an inkpot, and began.

But he very soon discovered
        that he couldn't write at all,
And his heart was filled with yearnings
        for a certain Mr Hall;
Till, after many years of doubt,
        he sent his friend a card:
'Have tried to write an Algebra,
        but find it very hard.'

Now Mr Hall himself had tried
        to write a book for schools,
But suffered from a handicap:
        he didn't know the rules.
So when he heard from Mr Knight
        and understood his gist,

He answered him by telegram:
        'Delighted to assist.'

So Mr Hall and Mr Knight
        they took a house together,
And they worked away at algebra
        in any kind of weather,
Determined not to give it up
        until they had evolved
A problem so constructed
        that it never could be solved.

'How hard it is,' said Mr Knight,
        'to hide the fact from youth
That x and y are equal:
        it is such an obvious truth!'
'It is,' said Mr Hall,
        'but if we gave a b to each,
We'd put the problem well beyond
        our little victims' reach.

Or are you anxious, Mr Knight,
        lest any boy should see
The utter superfluity
        of this repeated b?'
'I scarcely fear it,' he replied,
        and scratched his grizzled head,
'But perhaps it *would* be safer
        if to b we added z.'

'A brilliant stroke!' said Hall,
         and added z to either side;
Then looked at his accomplice
         with a flush of happy pride.
And Knight, he winked at Hall
         (a very pardonable lapse).
And they printed off the Algebra
         and sold it to the chaps.

Meet me in Usk
    And drone to me
Of what a beetle's
    Eye can see
When lamps are lit
And the bats flit
    In Usk
    At dusk.

And tell me if
    A beetle's nose
Detects the perfume
    Of the rose
As gardens fade
And stars invade
    The dusk
    In Usk.

Sir Smasham Uppe

Good afternoon, Sir Smasham Uppe!
We're having tea: do take a cup!
Sugar and milk? Now let me see –
Two lumps, I think? . . . Good gracious me!
The silly thing slipped off your knee!
Pray don't apologize, old chap:
A very trivial mishap!
So clumsy of you? How absurd!
My dear Sir Smasham, not a word!
Now do sit down and have another,
And tell us all about your brother –
You know, the one who broke his head.
Is the poor fellow still in bed? –
A chair – allow me, sir! . . . Great Scott!
That *was* a nasty smash! Eh, what?
Oh, not at all: the chair was old –
Queen Anne, or so we have been told.
We've got at least a dozen more:
Just leave the pieces on the floor.
I want you to admire our view:
Come nearer to the window, do;
And look how beautiful . . . Tut, tut!
You didn't see that it was shut?
I hope you are not badly cut!
Not hurt? A fortunate escape!
Amazing! Not a single scrape!

And now, if you have finished tea,
I fancy you might like to see
A little thing or two I've got.
That china plate? Yes, worth a lot:
A beauty too . . . Ah, there it goes!
I trust it didn't hurt your toes?
Your elbow brushed it off the shelf?
Of course: I've done the same myself.
And now, my dear Sir Smasham – Oh,
You surely don't intend to go?
You *must* be off? Well, come again.
So glad you're fond of porcelain!

A little party in the house –
The first to come is Mr Grouse.
And he has hardly settled down
When they announce Sir Fractious Frown;
And, just as talk is getting slack,
My Lord and Lady Answer Back.
This *is* a pleasure: I am proud.
Step in: you'll find we're quite a crowd.
And Mrs Contradict, I see,
Is just behind you: pardon me!
Another ring. Ah Lady Snap,
Permit me to remove your wrap.
How good of you to come so far
And bring the Grumbles in your car! –
Now bless my soul, I know that face!
And yet – of course, it's Miss Grimace.
These fashions alter people so!
Come in and take your hat off. No?
And who's this trotting up the stair?
Little Miss Quarrel, I declare!
So musical, so quick, so merry,
And clever with her fingers – very!
Ah Mr Bump, good afternoon!
I thought we might expect you soon.
Another knock. Dear Major Punch,
Most kind of you to rush your lunch!

Let me present Miss Whack. You've met her?
Old friends, you say? So much the better!
Lord Biff – allow me – Canon Batt.
At school together? Fancy that!
The world is really very small.
Excuse me – someone in the hall.
Aha, the gallant Captain Kick!
Late? Not at all. You're in the nick.
And you, Miss Shindy, come along:
We're counting on you for a song.
And now I think we're nearly done –
All here and happy – but for one.
Ah Mrs Tears, how *do* you do?
So glad you've brought your music too!
What dreadful weather! Do come in.
And now we might as well begin.

The Snake and the
Snake-Charmer

'Sing me to sleep,
    Light of me eyes!'
'Charmed!' said the Charmer,
    Wary and wise.

Classical airs,
    Handel and Brahms,
Anger the snake.
    So do the Psalms.

Sullivan's songs
    Over-excite;
Rachmaninoff
    Ends in a bite.

None but a jazz
    Melody charms
Flickering eyes
    Full of alarms.

Flickering eyes
    Drowsily close.
Odours of Ind
    Enter his nose –

Odours of India
　　Deep in the tune,
India perfumed
　　Under the noon.

The Hippopotamus's Birthday

He has opened all his parcels
        but the largest and the last;
His hopes are at their highest
        and his heart is beating fast.
O happy Hippopotamus,
        what lovely gift is here?
He cuts the string. The world stands still.
        A pair of boots appear!

O little Hippopotamus,
        the sorrows of the small!
He dropped two tears to mingle
        with the flowing Senegal;
And the 'Thank you' that he uttered
        was the saddest ever heard
In the Senegambian jungle
        from the mouth of beast or bird.

The Flattered Flying-Fish

Said the Shark to the Flying-Fish over the phone:
'Will you join me to-night? I am dining alone.
Let me order a nice little dinner for two!
And come as you are, in your shimmering blue.'

Said the Flying-Fish: 'Fancy remembering me,
And the dress that I wore at the Porpoises' tea!'
'How could I forget?' said the Shark in his guile:
'I expect you at eight!' and rang off with a smile.

She has powdered her nose; she has put on her things;
She is off with one flap of her luminous wings.
O little one, lovely, light-hearted and vain,
The Moon will not shine on your beauty again!

Meditations
of a Tortoise
Dozing under a Rosetree
near a Beehive
at Noon
while
a Dog
scampers about
and a Cuckoo calls
from a
Distant Wood

So far as I can see,
There is no one like me.

Tony the Turtle

Tony was a Turtle,
  Very much at ease,
Swimming in the sunshine
  Through the summer seas,
And feeding on the fishes
Irrespective of their wishes,
With a 'By your leave' and 'Thank you'
  And a gentlemanly squeeze.

Tony was a Turtle
  Who loved a civil phrase;
Anxious and obliging,
  Sensitive to praise.
And to hint that he was snappy
Made him thoroughly unhappy;
For Tony was a Turtle
  With most engaging ways.

Tony was a Turtle
  Who thought, before he fed,
Of other people's comfort,
  And as he ate them said:
'If I seem a little grumpy,
It is *not* that you are lumpy.'
  For Tony was a Turtle
  Delicately bred.

Peter and Percival

OR

The Penguins' Revolt

I

THE SUITORS

Peter and Percival lived in a place
Where the cold is too bitter for People to face,
But Peter and Percival both had contrived
To be Penguins, not People – and so they survived.

In their frozen abode at Antarctica's end
They not only flourished, but each had a friend;
For Fate, having made up her mind to be merciful,
Gave Percy to Peter and Peter to Percival.

Now Perce was a poet, a moulder of metre,
While prose was the medium chosen by Peter;
Yet Peter delighted in Percival's verse
And the prose of his Pete was as music to Perce.

This master of prose and this maker of rhyme
Adored the same lady, and both at a time;
For each, in his fashion, aspired to the hand
Of the Queen of the Penguins in Enderby Land.

When Peter and Perce were received at the Court,
Peter's proposal was painfully short,
For all he could say in the Presence was 'Yum!'
And it might have been better if he had been dumb.

Percy was equally wanting in tact,
Though endowed with the eloquence Peter had lacked;
For without having studied Her Majesty's views
He gaily committed himself to the Muse.

'What plumage!' he sang. 'What a beak! What a leg!
To think that such beauty came out of an egg!'
And he stopped for applause – in a silence complete
But for one little loyal explosion from Pete.

Her Majesty looked at the pair with a frown,
And remarked, as she primly adjusted her crown:
'Peter is pitiful; Percival worse:
We never have heard such indelicate verse!

Be off with you both, to discover the Pole.
And polish your style on the way to your goal,
Till Percy has learnt to add reason to rhyme,
And Pete to use more than a word at a time.'

Not a murmur from Pete, not a stanza from Percy,
No sighs of regret and no sueing for mercy,
But flipper in flipper they passed from her sight
Out under the stars of the Antarctic night.

THE REBELS

They had waddled a dismal disconsolate week
Before Percy recovered the use of his beak.
He blinked at the desolate acres of snow,
And moaned in his misery: 'Oh, what a go!'

'Is it sense,' he complained, 'is it fair, is it nice
To be banished for love over hummocky ice?
O Peterkin, Peter, have *you* any hope
Of Polar Discoveries?' Peter said: 'Nope!'

'And what if we penetrate into the South?
Is there anything there to put into one's mouth?
I once was a poet: at present I wish
For nothing so much as a – ' Peter said: 'Fish.'

'How apt! How concise! How deliciously put!'
Said Percival, scratching his head with his foot.
And he pondered a moment before he expressed
The emotions that flooded his feathery breast.

'I would like to be loyal, but since we were banished
My love for Her Majesty seems to have vanished.
I used to be charmed by her perfume and paint,
But just at the moment – ' Said Peter: 'You ain't.'

'And if, to put matters beyond any doubt,
I referred to Her Majesty's face as a snout –
If I ventured so far as to take such a step,
Would you follow me, Peterkin?' Peter said: 'Yep!'

'How perfect the pleasures of amity are!'
Said Perce, with his eye on a southerly star.
And they walked for a little, preoccupied each
With thoughts that refused to be put into speech.

'I observe you are ready,' said Perce, 'to rebel,'
When a hiccough from Peter had broken the spell.
'And if you are ready, then why should we wait?
Let us found a Reformed and Republican State!

With freedom to live as we jolly well please,
Freedom to hiccough, and freedom to sneeze,
Freedom for Poetry, freedom for Prose –
Let us dance the Democracy in with our toes!'

So they tripped in their glee through the star-spangled
Penguins in harmony, utterly right;   [night,
While the silent Aurora went flickering forth
And shivered the sky from the South to the North.

They danced their delight, in the star-sprinkled weather,
Peter and Percival, birds of a feather;
And the awful Aurora with shimmering hands
Shook her curtain out over the ice-covered lands.

We shared in one delightful house;
   We shared a mossy bed.
I never knew another mouse
   Than her – and she is dead.

The beady eye, the nimble strength,
   The soft and silken fur!
The whiskers, and the noble length
   Of tail that followed her!

And now I'm lonely in the run,
   And lonely on the stair,
And lonely in the nest we spun –
   So warm when she was there!

The wheel she loved to turn is still.
   The feet that ran so light
Have twinkled up the heavenly hill
   And tread the wheel of night.

*Soliloquy of a Tortoise
on Revisiting
the Lettuce Beds
after an Interval of One Hour
while supposed
to be
Sleeping
in a Clump
of Blue Hollyhocks*

One cannot have enough
Of this delicious stuff!

The Lesser Lynx

The laughter of the Lesser Lynx
    Is often insincere:
It pays to be polite, he thinks,
    If Royalty is near.

So when the Lion steals his food
    Or kicks him from behind,
He smiles, of course – but oh, the rude
    Remarks that cross his mind!

The Revoke

The Lion finds it difficult
               to get a game of cards
Since that unfortunate affair
               at Mrs Leo Pard's.
In vain he rings his hostess up
               in accents kind and hearty –
'They much regret . . . they cannot come . . .
               they have another party.'

Perhaps he *had* been hasty –
               he was certainly provoked
When his dainty little partner,
               Lady Antelope, revoked.
The Lion smiled and licked his chops
               in reminiscent vein –
'I'll wait till supper is announced,
               if I am asked again!'

The Albatross and the Equator

'Albatross, Albatross, why do you fly
Under my blue equatorial sky?
Albatross, Albatross, why do you roam
So far from your icy delectable home?'

'Capricorn warned me to turn to the right,
But I strayed from my course in the dead of the night;
And the stars of the tropics, so many and new,
Led me by long ways and weary to you.'

The kindly Equator arose with a yawn
To the green and gold of the tropical dawn.
He called his Leviathans, little and large,
And handed the Albatross into their charge.

And he said to his Porpoises: 'Cease from your play,
And listen to me for the rest of the day:
I never have seen and seldom have heard
Of such an amazingly beautiful bird.

She has flown from the far impossible South,
And strange are the sounds that come out of her mouth;
But the white of her breast and the spread of her wings
Are both surpassingly wonderful things.'

So they crowned her with seaweed Queen of the Birds
And humbly addressed her with flattering words;
And they gave her oysters and elegant fish
Daintily served on an amethyst dish.

They gave her a coral isle set in the calms
With a long white beach of coconut palms.
'Deign with your delicate feet,' said they,
'To tread this shade in the heat of the day.'

But the Albatross smiled with a tear in her heart,
As she said: 'I will walk for a little apart.'
And she paced by the echoing ocean alone,
Crooning a sorrowful song of her own:

'Fair are the tropical seas in the noon,
And fair in the glistening path of the moon.
But, oh, dearer to me are the storms of the Horn
Where the grey world-wandering waves are born.'

One moment they saw her, the next she had fled
Like a dream in the dawn or a shaft that is sped;
And all that she left on that desolate strand
Was the print of her foot and a tear in the sand.

She flew through the day and she flew through the night
With a heart that was bursting with hope and delight,
As the changing horizons came up with a swing
And the long leagues of ocean slipped under her wing –

Into the far incredible South,
Till she tasted the smell of the snow in her mouth,
And fluttered to rest in the land of her birth
On the ice that envelops the ends of the Earth.

The White Rabbit

He is white as Helvellyn when winter is well in;
  His whiskers are mobile and tender.
If it weren't for the greed that compels him to feed
  Without ceasing, his form would be slender.

With elegant hops he crushes or crops
  All the flowers that bloom in the garden;
Yet such is the grace that suffuses his face,
  He wins, without asking, our pardon.

The Sun, who rides heaven from Dover to Devon
  Inspecting furred folk and their habits,
Breaks out into poesy: 'What summer snow is he
  Made of, this pearl among rabbits?'

And at night on the lawn as he waits for the dawn,
  Rapt in dreams of a rabbit's perfection,
The Moon in her stride sweeps the cloudlets aside
  To rejoice in his silver reflection.

Night Thought
of a
Tortoise
Suffering from
Insomnia
on a Lawn

The world is very flat –
There is no doubt of that.

The Unicorn

The Unicorn stood, like a king in a dream,
On the bank of a dark Senegambian stream;
And flaming flamingoes flew over his head,
As the African sun rose in purple and red.

Who knows what the thoughts of a unicorn are
When he shines on the world like a visiting star;
When he comes from the magical pages of story
In the pride of his horn and a halo of glory?

He followed the paths where the jungle beasts go,
And he walked with a step that was stately and slow;
But he threw not a shadow and made not a sound,
And his foot was as light as the wind on the ground.

The lion looked up with his terrible eyes,
And growled like the thunder to hide his surprise.
He thought for a while, with a paw in the air;
Then tucked up his tail and turned into his lair.

The gentle giraffe ran away to relate
The news to his tawny and elegant mate,
While the snake slid aside with a venomous hiss,
And the little birds piped: 'There is something amiss!'

But the Unicorn strode with his head in a cloud
And uttered his innocent fancies aloud.
'What a wonderful world!' he was heard to exclaim;
'It is better than books: it is sweeter than fame!'

And he gazed at himself, with a thrill and a quiver,
Reflected in white by the slow-flowing river:
'Oh, speak to me, dark Senegambian stream,
And prove that my beauty is more than a dream!'

He had paused for a word in the midst of his pride,
When a whisper came down through the leaves at his
From a spying, malevolent imp of an ape   [side
With a twist in his tail and a villainous shape:

'He was made by the stroke of a fanciful pen;
He was wholly invented by ignorant men.
One word in his ear, and one puff of the truth –
And a unicorn fades in the flower of his youth.'

The Unicorn heard, and the demon of doubt
Crept into his heart, and the sun was put out.
He looked in the water, but saw not a gleam
In the slow-flowing deep Senegambian stream.

He turned to the woods, and his shadowy form
Was seen through the trees like the moon in a storm.
And the darkness fell down on the Gambian plain;
And the stars of the Senegal sought him in vain.

He had come like a beautiful melody heard
When the strings of the fiddle are tunefully stirred;
And he passed where the splendours of melody go
When the hand of the fiddler surrenders the bow.

Pirates on Funafuti

Full many a magic island
            lies within the seas of coral,
But only Funafuti wields
            a magic that is moral.
There is no island of the East
            or in the Spanish Main
That boasts a fauna so correct,
            a flora so urbane.

It is a pretty sight to see
            the billows doff their caps
In breaking on the beach,
            though this is natural perhaps.
The very coconuts that grow
            so slender in the glades
Incline politely to the winds,
            though these are only trades.

One sunny day a pirate band
            approached this happy shore,
Fresh from the looting of a ship,
            and looking out for more –
Jack Slaughter, Galapago Jim,
            Sam Stiff and Hairy Hugh,
Cuthbert the Cook and Barmy Bill –
            they *were* an ugly crew.

The first on Funafuti, as it fell,
    was Captain Jack,
Whom Sam in swinging round an oar
    had landed on his back.
And he rose up in the shallows
    with a murderous grimace –
When an unexpected simper
    altogether changed his face.

'Your pardon, Mr Stiff,' he said,
    'for being in the way.
The fault was mine entirely.
    Not another word, I pray.'
The crew were dumb. 'Be good enough
    to join me on the sand.
Come, Mr Galapago Jim.
    Allow me, Cook, a hand.'

The crew obeyed. They would have feared
    an angry lion less
Than this perplexing suavity,
    this painful *politesse*.
But as in turn they disembarked
    and caught the island's spell
Each felt an impulse to behave
    unusually well.

Said Jim, 'I happen to have brought
    a change in my valise.

Do me the honour, sir, I beg,
        of slipping into these.'
'Your kindly thought,' the Skipper said,
        'may well prevent a chill.
Excuse me for a moment.'
        And he went behind a hill.

And so in all propriety
        they dined upon the beach,
Restricting their consumption
        to a single helping each,
And choosing the right cutlery
        with cultivated ease
For caviare, asparagus,
        or macaroni cheese.

The evening's pleasure ended
        with a little tune from Sam.
'You cannot think,' the Captain said,
        'how deeply moved I am.
The moonlit scene, the tender words,
        my mother's favourite song –
I wonder, O my comrades,
        if a pirate's life is wrong!'

They led him sobbing to his bed,
        their own tears falling fast;
They tucked him in and held his hand
        until the fit had passed;

They smoothed his pillow neatly,
                    put his cutlass underneath,
And in a glass beside him
                    popped his artificial teeth.

Then one by one they said their prayers
                    and folded up their clothes,
Forgetful of the ribald jest,
                    the customary oaths;
And with a fairy tale or two
                    they talked themselves asleep
To the murmur of the palm-trees
                    and the gently stirring deep.

They sailed at dawn.
                    And as they left the magic coast behind,
The conduct of the company
                    immediately declined.
Their breakfast was a brutal thing;
                    at lunch they hardly spoke;
By dinner-time civility
                    was treated as a joke.

But still on Funafuti beach
                    the ocean rollers break
With a softly silenced thunder,
                    lest the little turtles wake;
Clams in their crannies hide their yawns;
                    and everything is done
To the perfect satisfaction
                    of the overseeing Sun.

The Green Train

The Blue Train for the South – but the Green Train for
Nobody knows when the Green Train departs.   [us.
Nobody sees her off. There is no noise; no fuss;
No luggage on the Green Train;
No whistle when she starts.
But quietly at the right time they wave the green light
And she slides past the platform and plunges into the
        night.

Wonderful people walking down the long Green Train,
As the engine gathers speed.
And voices talking.
'Where does she go to, Guard?'
Where indeed?
But what does it matter
So long as the night is starred?
Who cares for time, and who cares for the place,
So long as the Green Train thunders on into space?

'Misery me!'
Said the Lady of Leigh,
As she queued for a bus in the Strand,
And callous conductresses, weary of work,
Drifted disdainfully into the murk
With a laugh at her lily-white hand.
'Oh the ladylike ease at Leigh on the Sea!
The curtains and comfort, the toast and the tea!
There goes another one – misery me!
Misery me!'
Said the Lady of Leigh.

Bury her deep, down deep,
Safe in the earth's cold keep,
  Bury her deep –

No more to watch bird stir;
No more to clean dark fur;
No more to glisten as silk;
No more to revel in milk;
  No more to purr.

Bury her deep, down deep;
She is beyond warm sleep.
She will not walk in the night;
She will not wake to the light.
  Bury her deep.

Ian Serraillier

Ian Serraillier was born in London on 24 September 1912 and was educated at Brighton College and St Edmund Hall, Oxford. He is married and has four children, three girls and a boy. Before his marriage he travelled widely in Europe and is very fond of mountains (particularly Switzerland) and the sea. He prefers the country to the town and now lives in West Sussex in a flint house in the heart of the South Downs. He has taught in various schools – public schools and grammar schools – since 1935, and writing is only a spare-time occupation. His hobbies are walking, swimming, and climbing.

He has written the following books of verse for children: *Thomas and the Sparrow* (Oxford, 1946); *The Monster Horse* (Oxford, 1948); *The Ballad of Kon-Tiki* (Oxford, 1951); *Belinda and the Swans* (Cape, 1952); *Beowulf the Warrior* (Oxford, 1954); *Everest Climbed* (Oxford, 1956). His novels for children are: *They Raced for Treasure* (Cape, 1946); *Flight to Adventure* (Cape, 1947); *Captain Bounsaboard and the Pirates* (Cape, 1948); *There's No Escape* (Cape, 1950); *The Silver Sword* (Cape, 1956).

His educational books, published by Heinemann, include *Making Good*, *Jungle Adventure*, *The Adventures of Dick Varley*, and *Poems and Pictures*. Many of his poems have been broadcast and a serial based on his novel *The Silver Sword* has been broadcast in the B.B.C. Children's Television programme. He is founder and co-editor with his wife of the New Windmill series – a series of contemporary fiction for schools, published by Heinemann.

IAN SERRAILLIER, with a deep love of poetry and sensitive appreciation, approaches the task of composition as a craftsman. He does not catch inspiration from the air, but searches for it in personal experience. Sometimes, as in the case of his Everest Climbed, he deliberately acquires experience. Before he began to write it, he soaked himself for a year or more in all the relevant background material of heights and hazards, climbing and climbers, snow and ice.

He learned the technique of poetry-making at school, writing Latin and Greek verse, and has found that training valuable, the discipline sound and good, giving him a framework on which to lean while exploring effects and modes of expression.

As a schoolmaster he discovered how to recommend poetry to boys, and later to girls. He observed how they responded as he read aloud, and thought about the reasons for it. His conclusions as to the things that helped and those that hindered stimulated him to make experiments of his own to try out on those lively audiences. He chose some familiar tales and legends which everyone knows, retold and reshaped them, twisted some, wholly reclothed others, in the kind of language he knew would be acceptable. The results were vigorous, surprising, and stirring. His rhythms and verse forms were the more telling because the listeners expected the familiar, and discovered instead something entirely new in substance as well as form.

He writes positively for the spoken word. Perhaps all poets do – they must surely? But while for some – Eleanor Farjeon, for instance – the words are born singing themselves to a tune of their own, Ian Serraillier's spoken word is not something in the poet's head, so much as some reflection of the idiom of speech among those he writes for. He needs constantly to test and trim his work by those reactions.

He finds rhyme difficult, and definitely restrictive, so that he has sometimes gone through his work, deliberately removing the rhymes, and has found the effect obtained usually tauter and stronger. His style is ruggedly alive, and that ruggedness is part of his own personality – but part also of his conscious concern to make something boys and girls will accept readily, try out for themselves, and enjoy. He has recently been tackling vigorous and adventurous subjects – the story of Beowulf, the epic of the Kon-Tiki Expedition, the feat of the climbing of Everest.

He does not skimp the hard work necessary for the kind of thing he has chosen to do. As already mentioned, in order to write Everest Climbed, he first acquired all possible experience. He revived his own attempts at climbing, and set himself to feel and understand the tremendous realities of wind and bitter cold along with the technique of climbing. He studied background reports from all available sources – newspapers, films, personal accounts, B.B.C. studies, and so on. So he let the life and experiences of a climber come into his mind for a whole twelve months before he wrote a line – until he was able to move freely in that atmosphere, freely enough to think and write without restraint. Imagination, of course, plays a very great part in such work – imagination of that powerful quality which can reproduce such actualities truly and reliably, without exaggeration or distortion.

The Queens' Rhyme

The King has married *two* wives,
  Each a Prince's daughter.
'I'm a Queen, and you're a Queen,
  So who's to fetch the water?'

The Mouse in the Wainscot

Hush, Suzanne!
Don't lift your cup.
That breath you heard
Is a mouse getting up.

As the mist that steams
From your milk as you sup,
So soft is the sound
Of a mouse getting up.

There! did you hear
His feet pitter-patter,
Lighter than tipping
Of beads on a platter,

And then like a shower
On the window pane
The little feet scampering
Back again?

O falling of feather!
O drift of a leaf!
The mouse in the wainscot
Is dropping asleep.

Miss Tibbles is my kitten; white
As day she is and black as night.

She moves in little gusts and breezes
Sharp and sudden as a sneeze is.

At hunting Tibbles has no match.
How I like to see her catch

Moth or beetle, two a penny,
And feast until there isn't any!

Or, if they 'scape her, see her eyes
Grow big as saucers with surprise.

Sometimes I like her calm, unwild,
Gentle as a sleeping child,

And wonder as she lies, a fur ring,
Curled upon my lap, unstirring, –
Is it me or Tibbles purring?

The Kettle Rhyme

'My kettle's no use any more,' mother said,
    Misery you, misery me,
And she hurled the hole-y thing over the hedge.
    Misery diddle fa-la!

A robin who found it flew down from a tree:
    Merrily you, merrily me,
'This'll do nicely for missus and me.'
    Merrily diddle fa-la!

When father came home he was angry with mother:
    Misery you, misery me,
'I haven't the money to buy us another.'
    Misery diddle fa-la!

Now robin and family, happily settled,
    Merrily you, merrily me,
Peep out – all five – from the hole in the kettle.
    Merrily diddle fa-la!

The Hen and the Carp

Once, in a roostery
There lived a speckled hen, and when-
Ever she laid an egg this hen
Ecstatically cried:
'O progeny miraculous, particular spectaculous,
What a wonderful hen am I!'

Down in a pond nearby
Perchance a fat and broody carp
Was basking, but her ears were sharp –
She heard Dame Cackle cry:
'O progeny miraculous, particular spectaculous,
What a wonderful hen am I!'

'Ah, Cackle,' bubbled she,
'For your single egg, O silly one,
I lay at least a million;
Suppose for each I cried:
"O progeny miraculous, particular spectaculous!"
What a hullaballoo there'd be!'

Mrs Piper, tiny mite,
Had a giant's appetite;
She, as short as winter grass is,
Ate enough for twenty horses.
No, not even Humpty-Dumpty
Had so stretch-able a tumpty.
She ate so much when food was cheap
There wasn't any time to sleep;
When food was dear she slept all day
Or else, for lack, she pined away.
Peter, ere she'd vanished quite,
Found a pumpkin for his wife
Growing in a field alone.
He hollowed it into a home,
With door and window, leafy shutters,
Straw for pipes (in half for gutters).
Here they lived, whatever weather,
Long and happily together.
Fog or sunshine, storm or drizzle,
Peter sang while Mrs nibbled.
She never ate the pumpkin through –
The more she ate the more it grew.
Now, to end with, here's the song
That Peter sang – it isn't long:

Peter, Peter, Pumpkin-eater,
Had a wife and couldn't keep her.

He put her in a pumpkin shell
And there he kept her very well.

The Crooked Man

There was a crooked man was once a little lad,
He hadn't any mother and he hadn't any dad,
He hadn't any home or a family tree.
Where did he come from? Don't ask me.

This little crooked lad grew up to be a man
(One leg stopped where the other one began).
He hobbled with a stick for a whole crooked mile
And found a crooked sixpence upon a crooked stile.

He ran to a shop then – a-tinkle went the bell.
'Good morning to you, missus, and what do you sell?'
'I've candy and a barrow and a black silk hat.'
'None of those, thank you, I'll buy a crooked cat.'

He bought a crooked cat and it caught a crooked mouse
Pitter-patter down the gutter of an old farm-house.
'Be friends with me, mousie, there's no harm meant,
For we're all of us crooked here but me, and I'm bent.'

They jogged along together but they couldn't keep in
    step.
'Right turn!' said the crooked man – they turned to the
    left.
But he brought them at last to a little crooked house,
And he lived there for ever with the pussy and the mouse.

There was a crooked man and he walked a crooked mile,
He found a crooked sixpence upon a crooked stile.
He bought a crooked cat and it caught a crooked mouse,
And they all lived together in a little crooked house.

A gardener, Tobias Baird,
Sent his head to be repaired;
He thought, as nothing much was wrong,
He wouldn't be without it long.

Ten years he's weeded path and plot,
A headless gardener, God wot,
Always hoping (hope is vain)
To see his noddle back again.

Don't pity him for his distress –
He never sent up his address.

The Tale of Three Landlubbers

Once upon a time three landlubbers,
Sick of the daily grind,
Aching to be free,
Leapt into a boat and braved the wintry sea.

The first, a miller (he was pale as flour),
Said:
    'I'm fed up with choking in my mill
      Hour after dusty hour.
      I'd rather be dead.'
The second, a butcher (he was lean as Spratt),
Sighed:
    'Oh for a life without a wife,
      Without the nagging and the washing up
      For breakfast, dinner, tea and sup!
      I'm for a lush and lazy clime
      And would fain grow fat.'
The third, a sweep (and he was black as night),
cried:
    'Soot I detest!
      Not south I'd have us sail, nor east nor west,
      But north to the Arctic where it's always white.'

And so they sailed. Their courage sparkled bright
As the frosty stars. Their hopes were full
As the sail, high as the mountain mast,
And their hearts beat fast.
All went well – the sky was blue,

The sea calm, the cabin
Cosy as a kitten's purring.
All went well till the wind, bestirring,
Whipped up the swell and set the waves a-growling –
Down swept the tempest howling, howling.
The mast was split, the canvas rent,
The helm battered, and the oars
All of them bust or bent.
'Oh, what a mess!'
They cried. 'Back to land we go,
For there we suffered less!'
Limping, back they went.
They were lucky, though their hopes were shattered
And their courage spent.

The miller returned to his mill.
He's grinding there still.
As for the butcher, well, his wife
Was waiting for him with a stack
Of dishes, ceiling-high,
And a keen carving knife.
He went back.
He washed up.
She spared his life.
The sweep returned to his soot
And his dreams of the Arctic white.
He's black again from morn to night,
From head to foot.

And they all stayed put.

The Hare and the Tortoise

'You can't race me,' said Johnny the Hare,
'Before you've started I'll be there.
    From the barley field
    To the Farmer's barn
I'll lick you, Sammy, fair and square.'

Sammy the Tortoise said, 'Wait and see!'
Away he crawled to his family (three),
    Clarence, Creeper,
    And Marmaduke –
They were alike as like could be.

'I've entered, mi-lads, for a steeplechase.
I can't leap over the land apace,
    But if four of us run
    Disguised as one,
I guess I can win this jolly old race.

'Clarence, you hide by the green duck pond;
Creeper, in pigsty a mile beyond.

'The starting line, yon barley stook,
Is just the place for you, Marmaduke.

'And me? I'll hide where I'm needed most
A nose and a half from the winning-post.'

Marm and Johnny lined up at the start.
'This race,' said Johnny, 'is really a farce.
    The wheat I sow
    From my bag as I go
Will be ready to cut by the time you pass.'

Bang! – they're off! The Hare at a bound
Rocketed over the billowy ground.
    But when he skirted
    The green duck pond,
The Tortoise was only a yard behind.

And when he came to the old pigsty
They were almost neck and neck – O my!

Poor Johnny the Hare, his field half sown,
Threw off his bag and continued alone,
    Drooping and dropping
    And stooping and stopping
And puffing and panting, terribly blown.

Ten yards from the tape he grew a bit bolder
And casting a careless eye over shoulder,
    'Sam, are you there?'
    Said Johnny the Hare.
'I've won!' said the Tortoise, in front, 'I told yer.'

Farmer and friends were holding the tape,
And *there* was Sammy, all bowing and scrape,

His head held high –
What a sock in the eye
For Johnny, who stands with his mouth agape.

'Well done!' said the Farmer. 'And now, methinks,
'Tis proper to offer you eats and drinks.
    Will you join me, both?'
    'No!' with an oath
Said Johnny the Hare, and home he slinks.

But later back to the farm he hobbled;
His limbs were still limp, and his brain was fuddled.
As he peered through the window he babbled and
    Bubbled:
    '*Four* Sammies I see
    A-sipping their tea!
    Strikes me
I galloped so fast I'm seeing twice double.'

The Fox Rhyme

Aunt was on the garden seat
   Enjoying a wee nap and
Along came a fox! teeth
   Closed with a snap and
He's running to the woods with her
   A-dangle and a-flap and –
Run, uncle, run
   And see what has happened!

Death of the Cat

Alas! Mowler, the children's pride,
Has slipped on a water-butt, tumbled inside
And died.

The seamstress on her sewing machine
Stitched a shroud of satin sheen.

The carpenter hammered and planed a coffin
Of seasoned oak without a knot in.

The sexton – he loved dear Mowler well –
Mournfully, mournfully tolled the bell.

Few were the prayers the parson spoke.
All he could do, poor fellow, was choke.

But saddest of all in the funeral train
Were the children. Deep were their sorrow and pain,

For they knew, as they followed the churchyard through,
They'd never set eyes on Mowler again.

In silence behind the coffin they stepped,
Solemnly, slowly. Everyone wept

Except
The little mice hid in the hedge – not they!

'Twas not *their* hearts that bled.
'Let's out and play,'
They cried. 'Oh, spread
The butter thick on the bread!
Dance in cream cheese right up to our knees,
For the cat is dead!
Hooray!
The cat
       is
           dead!'

Girls and Boys, Come out to Play

Girls and boys, come out to play!
The moon doth shine as bright as day,
So leave your supper and leave your slate,
Susan, Peter and Paul and Kate –
Are you coming?
Head over heels they leapt from bed,
And Tarry Awhile and Sleepyhead
Crept from the bench in the chimney nook.
The children came from the picture books,
Little Jack Horner, Miss Bo-peep –
'Somebody please look after my sheep!' –
Red Riding Hood hot from the wolf in the wood,
And baby Helen would come if she could.
(Who's Helen, you ask? Helen's my daughter.
Blue eyes, white hair, she's only a quarter.)
Jack and Jill and Margery Daw,
Miss Muffet, the spider, and Punch and more
Came with a shout, came with a bound
And danced in the moonlight round and round.

What shall we play till break of day,
Mulberry Bush or Nuts and May?
Said the owl in the willow, 'Tuwhit, tuwhoo!
I'm game to hunt the slipper or shoe,'
But as nobody offered a shoe or slipper
They had to do with a breakfast kipper,
Which answered well till it made a mess

Of Miss Muffet's beautiful blue print dress.
O come with a whistle, come with a call,
Come with a will or come not at all!
Who's clattering there? It's Old Mother Hubbard
Playing Grandmother's Footsteps in front of her cup-
board.
'Any pies?' said Horner. Old Mother said, 'None!'
But he put in his finger and pulled out a plum.
Up the ladder and down the wall,
A half-penny roll will serve us all:
But Jack rolled right from the top of the hill
And cracked his crown, and so did Jill.

Now for another game – what do you think
Of Hide and Seek or Tiddlywink,
Oranges and Lemons (oh for a taste!)
Or Follow My Leader? – hold on to my waist,
Through moon-white woods we'll twist and twine –
Now, Margery Daw, don't break the line.
But Margery stopped to play Pig in the Middle
With the dish and the spoon while the cat played the
fiddle.
And the tail swept onward, on with a bound
To the windmill, over the river and round,
Till Wee Willie Winkie overhead
As he flew in the sky, in the witch-way, said:
'You children ought to be in bed!'

Girls and boys, go home to rest –
Jenny Wren's asleep in her nest,

The owl has floated back to his willow,
Punch is using his hump as a pillow.
The sleepy children droop and drop,
Unwound as weary spinning top,
And crawl to bed. Miss Bo-peep
(No sheep) is sobbing herself to sleep,
While downstairs huddle into a corner
Miss Muffet, spider, Little Jack Horner.
Open the door, you'll see Mother Hubbard
Curled up like a cat, top shelf in her cupboard.

Lastly, dragging leg on leg,
Tarry Awhile and Sleepyhead,
Dozing, climb the window through,
Stretch and yawn . . . . . I'm sleepy too
And wonder, in the moonlight gleaming
What is baby Helen dreaming? . . . . .
Sssh!
      Don't wake her.
            Good night.

The Tickle Rhyme

'Who's that tickling my back?' said the wall.
'Me,' said a small
  Caterpillar. 'I'm learning
  To crawl.'

The Squirrel

Among the fox-red fallen leaves I surprised him. Snap
Up the chestnut bole he leapt,
The brown leaper, clawing up-swept:
Turned on the first bough and scolded me roundly.
That's right, load me with reviling,
Spit at me, swear horrible, shame me if you can.
But scared of my smiling
Off and up he scurries. Now Jack's up the beanstalk
Among the dizzy giants. He skips
Along the highest branches, along
Tree-fingers slender as string,
Fur tail following, to the very tips:
Then leaps the aisle –
O fear he fall
A hundred times his little length!
He's over! clings, swings on a spray,
Then lightly, the ghost of a mouse, against the sky traces
For me his runway of rare wonder, races
Helter-skelter without pause or break
(I think of the snail – how long would he take?)
On and onward, not done yet –
His errand? Some nut-plunder, you bet.
Oh he's gone!
I peer and search and strain for him, but he's gone.

I wait and watch at the giants' feet, among
The fox-red fallen leaves. One drop

Of rain lands with a smart tap
On the drum, on parchment leaf. I wait
And wait and shiver and forget. . . .

A fancy: suppose these trees, so ancient, so
Venerable, so rock-rooted, suddenly
Heaved up their huge elephantine hooves
(O the leaves, how they'd splutter and splash
Like a waterfall, a red waterfall) – suppose
They trudged away!
What would the squirrel say?

The Ballad of Kon-Tiki

THE RAFT

All day the plane had searched for them, the wild
Kon-Tiki sailors on their brittle raft,
In vain: circling the world from sea rim to sea rim,
Diving down through the boisterous cloud to find
No land anywhere, no sign of raft
Or any living thing, only
The foam-white wave in a wilderness of water
And a wilderness of hope.

                                  What need of a plane?
It's easier for *you* to find them.
Plunge with me now through the cloud – if you dare –
And with an eagle eye pin-point
One flake of foam darker than the rest.
That's the raft, d'you see it? – tiny, frail
As a rose petal blown on a stormy lake.
Drop closer now. Hover over the wave
Till you feel the sting of salt. It's not so frail
As it looks, that raft. Nine logs of balsa wood
Lashed side to side, pointed
With splashboards at the prow;
For mast two mangrove stems tied at the top;
A bamboo yard with four-corner sail painted
With Kon-Tiki's bearded face, Kon-Tiki son of the Sun;
Behind him the cane cabin, plaited with reed
And tiled with banana leaf, a ramshackle tool-shed thing

That creaks in every wind. This was their home
For a hundred days, this wooden tray, this balsa platter,
This cork steamroller snubbing the cheeky wave,
Now riding the mountain crest, now swamped
And swallowed, a sieve to each falling sea.

Six men lived here: the skipper,
Thor Heyerdahl of Norway who planned the game,
Confident, courageous as the god
Who gave him his name – he's at the helm now,
Tugging at the tiller in the climbing sea;
Torstein Raaby, merry and resourceful,
A wizard in wireless – d'you see him there
Crouched in the corner with earphones plastered
On his yellow stubble hair,
Tapping out a message with battery and box?
(Don't touch him for fear of electric shocks);
And Knut beside him, brave Knut of Norway –
You'll hear soon how he saved them from disaster;
Danielsson of Sweden, cook and quartermaster,
Professor with a flaming beard
That seemed to scorch his face, most learned about fish,
Placid in peril – look at him,
Sprawled on the cabin floor with his beard in a book.
He doesn't notice how the raft reels and rocks
But calmly reads on and on and on –
There are seventy more books in his stock;
Herman Watzinger, weather boss and boatswain –
Is there a tougher man alive?
He broke his neck at Lima and survived.

Lastly, Erik Hesselberg, a burly fellow
Broad as a barn door and full of fun,
He was everything rolled into one:
Navigator, splicer, sail-patcher, wood-carver,
Draughtsman and painter, hulking hula dancer –
And he could play the mandolin
And sing:
  'Violée violà violée-li-lillio
    The breadboard's a-bobbing on the wild wet sea
    O the whale and the shark they can nibble her like
      billy-o
    And swaller all the others – but they won't get me!'
And there was a green parrot in a cage,
A real smarty who with one tweak of his beak
Could twist the doorknob and vanish,
And if you chased him swear at you in Swedish
And in Spanish.
Six men, a parrot, and a small tame crab
Whose name was Johnny; he lived in a hole near the
    steering block
And came when he was called.

The Ballad of Kon-Tiki

They were not lonely. They found the sea
No barren waste but a living world,
Peopled as the woodland with wild creatures,
Curious and shy. The rough-riding steamer
With his foaming prow and his engine roar
Sees them not. But Kon-Tiki scared them not away.
As timid birds at twilight hop and twitter
On the summer lawn about the quiet house,
So now about the noiseless floating raft
The frolicking sea-dwellers. Then did Ocean,
The great showman, out of the bountiful deep
Conjure all manner of strange creatures
To delight them: flying fish that shot through the air
Like quicksilver, smack against the sail,
Then dropped to deck into the breakfast saucepan
Waiting there; the prosperous tunny,
Fat as an alderman with rows of double chins;
The glorious dolphin, bluebottle-green
With glittering golden fins, greedy
For the succulent weed that trailed like garlands
From the steering oar. There were many more –
Take the blue shark, a glutton
For blood; he'd swallow a dolphin, bones and all,
And crunch them like a concrete-mixer. They learnt
How to fool him with tit-bits, to get him

By his tail and haul aboard, skipping
Quickly from the snapping jaw –
He'd make a meal of anyone who let him!
(Rare sport this for the parrot who
For safety flew to the roof of the raft
And shrieked at the fun of it and laughed and laughed.)
Every kind they saw, from the million pilot fish
Tiny as a finger nail
To the majestic tremendous spotted whale,
Long as a tennis-court, who could –
Were he so minded – with one flick of his great tail
Have swatted them flat as a fly. But he couldn't be
    bothered.
Instead, circling cumbrously below,
He scratched his lazy back on the steering oar,
Till Erik sent him packing
With half a foot of steel in his spine.
Deep down he plunged, and the harpoon line –
Whipping through their hands – snapped like twine.

These marvels were the day's. What words
Can paint the night,
When the sea was no darkness but a universe of light?
Lo, in their wake a shoal
Of little shrimps, all shining,
A sprinkle of red coal!
Drawn by the gleaming cabin lamp, the octopus,
The giant squid with green ghostly eyes,
Hugged and hypnotized;
While, fathoms below, in the pitch-black deep were gliding

Balloons of flashing fire, silver
Streaming meteors. O world of wonder!
O splendid pageantry!
Hour after dreamy hour they gazed spell-bound,
Trailing their fingers in the starry sea.

THE ICEFALL

It was April when they came to the Icefall – Hillary,
His coolies and Sherpas, fifty strong.
In the forest of ice they camped, upon Khumbu,
In the white moon-world where no grass, nothing
    grew.
And the snow fell all day long. They were cold
And wet, some of them snow-blinded,
Short of tents and shelter – but nobody minded.
With the weather at freezing (or a shade below)
They turned their backs to the wind, crouched behind
    boulders and stones,
Or lay content as huskies, curled in the snow.
Next morning, when the snow had done with falling,
They kicked their way through the crust. And the
    climbers
Plodded on till, turning the valley head, they beheld
A white cascade of water, waves down the mountain
Leaping and whirling! But the giant fountain
In frosty plunge appalling
Had frozen, to silence quelled, cold as the tomb.
It was the Icefall, grim guardian of the Western Cwm,
The green-white monster with a hundred mouths
And jaws abysmal and fangs of ice. Near the way
Of the avalanche he lay,
Sprawled between Lhotse and Nuptse, sleepy-seeming,

Till down from those bastions the thunder came scream-
    ing
In billow-cloud of snow, with loud echoes in the summits
    booming
And rumbling, booming and rumbling. And boulders of
    ice collided,
Split to a million pieces which the yawning mouths
    devoured,
Groaning for more. Now upon their greed a white spray
    subsided,
While from deep caverns and creeks
Slowly the silence and the fear
Surged back. . . . But Hillary looked aloft and raised a
    cheer –
For April was sweeping the snow from the peaks!

Then Hillary attacked. Snow falling, wind howling,
Five days he fought, with axe and hoisting gear,
Ladder of aluminium, ladder of rope
And timber for bridging. Time and again
They were beaten back –
When cliff and wall crumbled, when avalanche
Wiped out a hundred feet of track,
By crevasse and gaping chasm, by toppling pinnacle
And serac overhanging. But they fought back.
Hack, hack at the ice! Over that ridge now –
Here's a flag to mark it – keep to the left of this –
We'll fix a line to the wall there – watch for the abyss.
Hack, hack at the ice! It was the same every day
Till they pitched a couple of tents on a shelf half way.

Hack, hack at the ice! More ridges,
Crevasses and pinnacles and chasms and bridges.
Hack, hack at the ice! or wade in the snow knee-deep
And battle to the top. At 20,000 there was room,
Just room to pitch a tent and, over the brink above, peep
Into their dreams and longings, into the Western Cwm.

One November morning clean and cold, 43

Peter and Percival lived in a place, 125
Poor Crusoe saw with fear-struck eyes, 81
Poor Jane Higgins, 63

Rise harrow, rake harrow, 40
Run a little this way, 58

Said the Shark to the Flying-Fish over the phone, 122
She took a last and simple meal when there were none to see her
    steal, 102
'Sing me to sleep, 119
Sleeping in the big bed, 110
Slowly the tide creeps up the sand, 56
Smooth and flat, grey, brown and white, 57
So far as I can see, 123
Some time! some time! 17
Stocking and shirt, 78

The Blue Train for the South – but the Green Train for us, 145
The buttercups in May, 55
The furry moth explores the night, 85
The house that we live in was built in a place, 107
The King has married *two* wives, 153
The laughter of the Lesser Lynx, 131
The Lion finds it difficult to get a game of cards, 132
The Sea is a hungry dog, 82
The tide in the river, 29
The Unicorn stood, like a king in a dream, 138
The world is very flat, 137
There met two mice at Scarborough, 69
There was a crooked man was once a little lad, 160
There was a man of Uriconium, 92
There was a yellow pumpkin, 46